Blue-Tailed Horse

The Laidlaw Reading Program LEVEL 5

William Eller
Kathleen B. Hester

S. Elizabeth Davis

Thomas J. Edwards

Roger Farr

Jack W. Humphrey

DayAnn McClenathan

Nancy Lee Roser

Elizabeth M. Ryan

Ann Myra Seaver

Marian Alice Simmons

Margaret Wittrig

Patricia J. Cianciolo, *Children's literature*

David W. Reed, *Linguistics*

LAIDLAW BROTHERS • PUBLISHERS

A Division of Doubleday & Company, Inc.

RIVER FOREST, ILLINOIS

Irvine, California   Chamblee, Georgia   Dallas, Texas   Toronto, Canada

Acknowledgments

Thomas Y. Crowell Company, Inc., for "A Robin." From FEATHERED ONES AND FURRY by Aileen Fisher. Copyright © 1971 by Aileen Fisher. With permission of Thomas Y. Crowell Company, Inc., publisher.

Garrard Publishing Company for "Whistle" by B. J. Lee. From ALL ABOUT ME selected by Leland B. Jacobs © 1971. With permission of Garrard Publishing Company.

Kids' Publishers, Inc., for "Popcorn" by Janet M. Perry and "The Fox" by Margaret Hannon. Reprinted from KIDS, *The Magazine by Kids for Kids*, Issue #5, Copyright 1971 by Kids' Publishers, Inc.

J. B. Lippincott Company for "What Someone Said When He Was Spanked on the Day Before His Birthday." From the book YOU KNOW WHO by John Ciardi. Copyright, © 1964 by John Ciardi. Reprinted by permission of J. B. Lippincott Company.

Parents' Magazine Enterprises, Inc., for use of the ideas underlying the following stories: "The Talking Crow," by Ann Devendorf, from the February, 1970, issue of HUMPTY DUMPTY; "Get Up and Shut the Door," by Sally Jarvis, from the May, 1970, issue of HUMPTY DUMPTY; "The Horse with the Blue Tail," by Richard Tyler, from the March, 1967, issue of HUMPTY DUMPTY.

Review Publishing Company for use of the idea underlying the story "The Thing at the End of the Line" by Delores Paulson. From *Child Life*, Copyright © 1969. Review Publishing Company.

Project Director: Ralph J. Cooke
Senior Editor: Helen W. Crane
Editor: Barbara Ryan
Production Director: LaVergne Niequist
Production Editors: Katherine Rossow, Angela Zabransky
Art Director: Gloria Muczynski
Art Consultants: Donald Meighan, Don Walkoe
Cover Art: Donald Charles
Illustrators: Angela Adams, Marc Belenchia, Robert Binks, Robert Borja, Ted Carr, Deso Csanady, Betty Fraser, Ruth Hoffman, John Magine, Larry Mikec, Krystyna Orska, Joe Rogers, Sylvie Selig, Hans Zander
Photographers: Robert Buchbinder (pp. 39, 53, 105, 120-121, 152, 154-155, 191); Bill Rogers (p. 153)

ISBN 0-8445-3146-4

Contents

Pets and Things

Page

Heads and Tails

Feet and Wings

Turnips and Kings

A Big Day for Charly

This was the day.

The day to go fishing.

Charly went to look for Dad.

"Will you go with me?" she asked.

"Go where?" asked Dad.

"You know!" said Charly.
"I want to go fishing.
This is the day to go!
Will you go with me?"

"I would like to go with you," said Dad.

"But I can't go now.

 Have you asked Grandpa?

 He likes to fish."

"Grandpa will go!" said Charly.

"I know he will."

Charly ran to see Grandpa.

"Would you like to go fishing?"
she asked.

"We can go to the pond."

"I would like to go," said Grandpa.

"But I can't do it now."

Then he looked at Charly.

"Why do you want to go to the pond?"
he asked.

"There are no fish in it."

"I like the pond," said Charly.
"Why are there no fish in it?"

"You will see," said Grandpa.
"Some day I will go fishing with you.
But not at the pond."

"I would like to go now," said Charly.
"This is just the day for fishing."

"Some day we will go," said Grandpa.
"But not now."

"Who wants to go fishing some day?"
asked Charly.

"Not me!

I want to go now."

"You can go now,"
said Charly's mother.
"Take this with you.

Just don't fish all day."

"M-m-m-m!" said Charly.
"I will have this
when I am fishing."

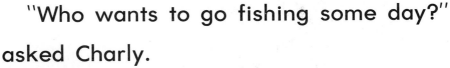

13

At the Pond

Charly ran down to the pond.

When she got there

she sat,

and sat,

· and sat.

Charly saw a  and a green .

But she did not see a fish.

Not one.

14

Charly did not stop fishing.

She sat and looked at the 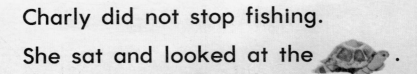 .

"I guess the fish don't like this pond,"
she said.

"Oh, I do want to get a fish.

Just one!

I want . . .

A fish!

I got one.

I got a fish."

"I want Grandpa to see this,"
said Charly.

"He said there are no fish
in the pond.

I guess he will come here now."

"Hey, Grandpa," called Charly.
"Guess what I got!"

But Grandpa did not have to guess.
He saw what Charly had.
"It can't be!" he said.
"It just can't be!"

What can Charly do with the fish?
Will Grandpa go fishing
at the pond now? Why?

Chester

Betsy had a dog.

She called the dog Chester.

Betsy had a wagon, too,
and a bike.

Betsy liked to play with Chester,
and the bike,
and the wagon.

18

One day Chester got in the wagon.

He was a big dog,

but he was not too big

for the wagon.

Betsy got on her bike.

"OK, Chester,"

she called.

"Here we go!"

Away they went . . .

Chester in the wagon,

and Betsy on her bike.

Betsy said, "Chester is big.

He can pull the wagon."

Did Chester pull the wagon?

No, he did not!

He just sat.

That is all he would do.

Can Betsy get Chester to pull
the wagon?

What will she do?

Run, Chester, Run

Peter liked to play with Chester, too.

One day he said, "Chester is big.

Can he pull the wagon

with my  in it?"

"Let's see," said Betsy.

Away ran Chester with the

in the wagon.

Peter and Betsy ran, too.

At last Betsy said, "Get in, Peter.

Chester is big.

He can pull you."

When Peter got in the wagon,

he called, "OK, Chester.

Let's go."

Did Chester pull the wagon?

No!

All he did was sit.

"Come on, Chester," said Betsy.

"Don't just sit there.

Get up and run."

But Chester would not run.

He would not get up.

He just sat

and looked around.

At last Peter asked,

"What will we do?"

24

"I know!" said Betsy.

"Take out the 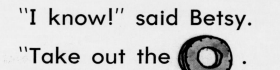 .

Then Chester will run."

Did Chester want to run?

No!

He just wanted to sit

and look around.

25

"Now what?" asked Peter.

"You get out," said Betsy.

Peter jumped out of the wagon.
He looked at Chester.

Chester looked at Peter.
Then he looked at Betsy.

26

At last Chester ran.

He ran fast.

Why did Chester run?

Something for Sara

"Sara, come here," called her mother.
"Come here.
 Fast!"

"Oh, oh," said Sara.
 She jumped up and ran to her mother.

"What did I do now?" she asked.

"Just look at your clothes,"
said Sara's mother.
"They are here and there
and all around."

Sara looked down.
She wished she had not come.

"We have to do something,"
said her mother.
"Some of your old clothes
will have to go."

"Why?" asked Sara.

"Some of your old clothes are too little," said her mother.

"Put this on and you will see."

Sara put on the yellow .

"I guess it is too little," she said.

Mother looked at all of the clothes.

"We can give away the ones
that are too little," she said.
"But some of your clothes are too old
to give away."

Sara put on a red .
"We can't give this away,"
she said.

"What will we do
with the old clothes?"
asked Sara.

"I don't know,"
said her mother.
"Give them to me now.
Some day I will make something
out of them."

She went away with the clothes,
and Sara ran out to play.

What can Sara's mother make
out of the old clothes?

What Is It?

The next day Sara's mother did not go away to work.

She got out the old clothes and looked at them.

"They are too little and too old," she said.

"But I can make something out of them."

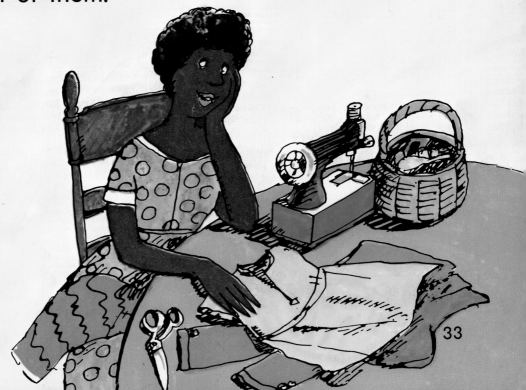

33

Sara's mother went to work
on the old clothes.

She went snip-snip here
and snip-snip there.

Next she made something
that was big and long.
It looked like this.

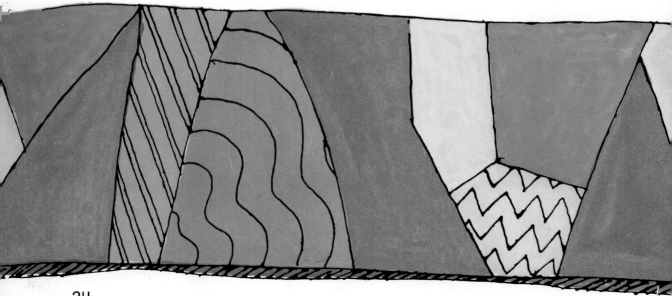

When Sara came in from play,
she asked, "What is that?"

"Something for you," said Mother.
"I went snip-snip here
and snip-snip there.
Then I made something big and long."

"What will it be?" asked Sara.

"You will see when it is all made,"
said her mother.

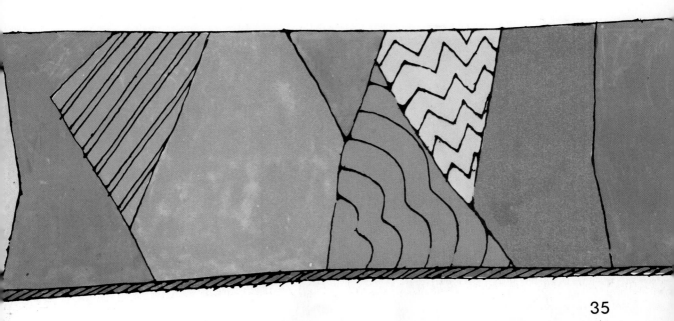

Then one day Sara's mother called,
"Sara, I want you."

"What now?" asked Sara.
But she came in from play.

"I made something for you,"
said her mother.
"I made it big.
I made it long.
I put a  on it.
Can you guess
what it is?"

36

"Oh, I can't guess!"
laughed Sara.
"Let me see, Mother.
Where is it?"

"I put it in there,"
said her mother.
"Go and see.
Then you will know."

37

"Oh, Mother! Mother!" called Sara.
"You did make something for me."

Then she laughed.
"Let's call it Wiggles."

What did Sara's mother do
to make Wiggles?
What can Sara do with Wiggles?

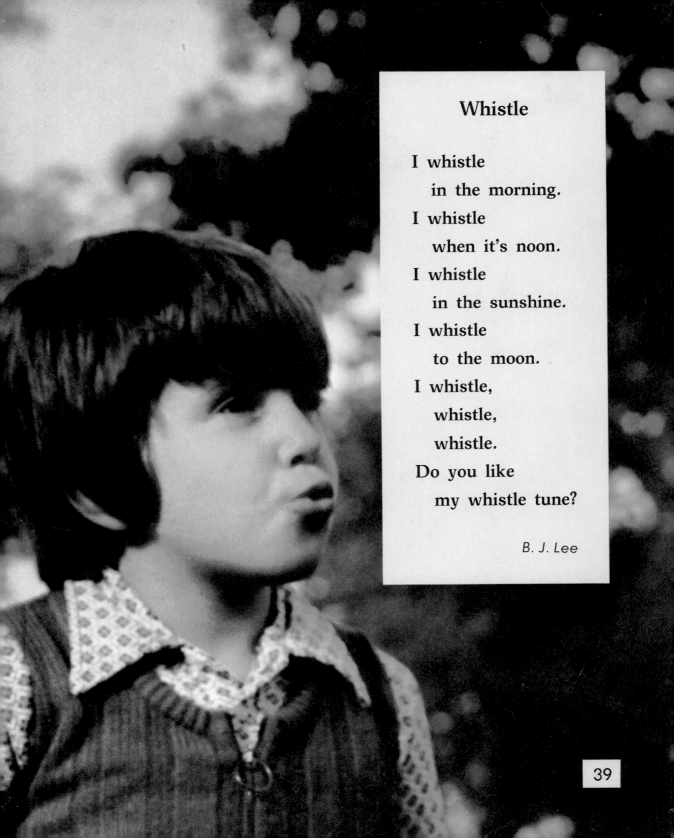

Whistle

I whistle
   in the morning.
I whistle
   when it's noon.
I whistle
   in the sunshine.
I whistle
   to the moon.
I whistle,
   whistle,
   whistle.
Do you like
   my whistle tune?

B. J. Lee

The Run Away

Stevie was going to run away.

He had on his old clothes—

the ones he liked to play in.

He had a box, too,

with something in it.

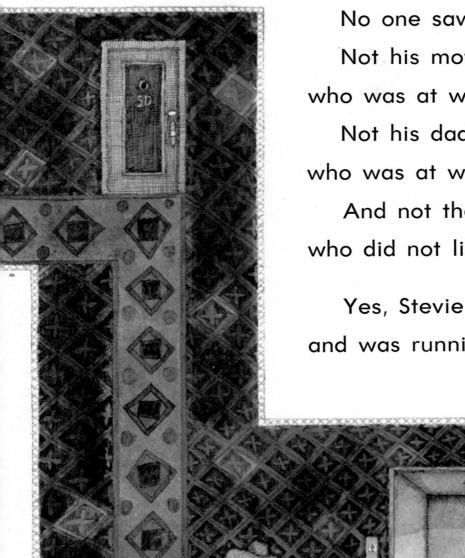

No one saw Stevie go.

Not his mother,

who was at work.

Not his dad,

who was at work, too.

And not the sitter,

who did not like Stevie.

Yes, Stevie had his box

and was running away.

When Stevie got on the elevator,
he saw Mark.

"What are you doing?"
asked Mark.

"Running away,"
said Stevie.
"No one knows.
Not my mother.
Not my dad.
Not my sitter.
Just you."

They went down in the elevator.
Mark looked at Stevie.

"I know what to do
when you run away,"
he said.
"I do it all the time.
Do you want me
to go with you?"

"I would like that,"
said Stevie.

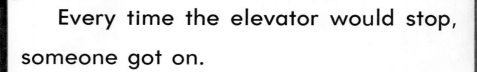

Every time the elevator would stop,
someone got on.

Everyone looked at the box.

Something in it went

up and down,

up and down,

up and down.

"What's in your box?" asked Mark.

"Sh!" said Stevie.

Egbert

A man got on at the next stop.

The box went up and down.
Everyone just looked.
Then out of the box jumped
a little white mouse.

"A mouse!" said someone.
"There is a mouse running around
on this elevator!"

"Egbert!" called Stevie.
"Get back in your box."

Egbert did not like the box.
He would not go back in it.
The little white mouse
looked all around.
Then . . .

He went up, up, up.
Up someone's leg.
And into his [pocket].

"Get out!" said the man.
"Get out of my [pocket]."

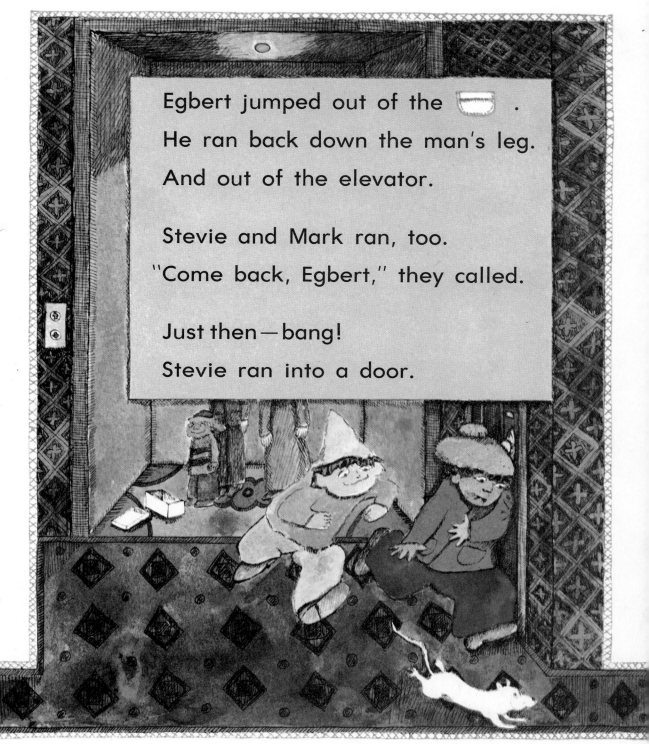

Egbert jumped out of the .

He ran back down the man's leg.

And out of the elevator.

Stevie and Mark ran, too.

"Come back, Egbert," they called.

Just then—bang!

Stevie ran into a door.

The door made Stevie stop.
But it did not stop Egbert.

Stevie got up.
"Egbert, come here," he called.

Egbert did not come.
He ran back into the elevator.
Now it was going up.

"What?" asked the man.
"Are you here again?"

He looked around and he saw the box.
"I guess you came out of here,"
he said.

So the man put Egbert into the box.
Then he went out of the elevator.

Where Is Egbert?

Mark said, "Come on, Stevie.
We are running away.
You don't have to take Egbert."

So Mark and Stevie got back
in the elevator.

Stevie said, "Now I will never see
my white mouse again."

Just then Egbert jumped out
of his box.

Up Stevie's leg he ran.

And into his .

This is where he wanted to be.

"Egbert!" said Stevie.

"You never did like that box.

You came back just in time.

Now we can run away."

"Not me!" said Mark.

"I have to go now."

"I do too," said Stevie.

"Dad will be looking for me.

Let's run away again some time."

Why did Stevie want to run away?

What Someone Said
When He Was Spanked
on the Day Before His Birthday

Some day

I may

Pack my bag and run away.

Some day

I may.

But not today.

Some night

I might

Slip away in the moonlight.

I might.

Some night.

But not tonight.

Some night.

Some day.

I might.

I may.

But right now I think I'll stay.

John Ciardi

53

How to Make a Parachute

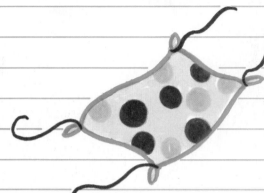

This is what you do.

1. Tie strings to the corners of a handkerchief.

2. Tie the strings to a stick.

3. Then, roll up the parachute.

Throw the parachute up.

It will look like this.

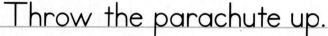

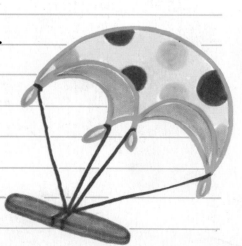

Heads and Tails

One Cold Day

Old Man: **Br-r-r-r!**

It is cold out there.

Old Woman: **I guess it is, Old Man.**

Old Man: **It is cold in here, too.**

56

Old Woman:　Shut the door.

Then you will not be cold.

Old Man:　I shut the door last.

You do it this time.

Old Woman:　Get up, Old Man.

Don't just sit there.

Get up and shut the door.

Old Man:　No!

I did it last time.

Old Woman: Br-r-r-r!

I will not shut the door.

You will not shut the door.

Who will do it then?

Old Man: I know!

The first one to talk

will have to do it.

He will talk first.
I know he will.

She will be
the first
to talk.

58

Who Will Talk First?

Mother Hen: Ooh! Ooh!

We are cold out here.

Can we come in?

Now she will talk.
She will talk first.

I will not be
the first one
to talk.

Old Man looks at Old Woman.
Old Woman looks at Old Man.
They do not talk.

Mother Hen: No one said "Yes."
No one said "No."
Come in chicks.
No one will stop us.

Chick One: Go away.

               That's my corn.

Chick Two: I don't want to go away.

               I saw the corn first.

Mother Hen: Stop that, you two chicks!

               There is corn for all of us.

Chick Three: OK!

               Then give me some corn.

Old Man: Get away from here.

All of you.

Out! Out! Out!

[
Old Man talks.

Mother Hen runs out of the door.

The three chicks run, too.
]

Old Woman: Now you will have
to shut the door.

Old Man: Oh, I will.
I give up!

[
Old Man gets up.
He shuts the door.
Old Man and Old Woman laugh.
]

Why did Old Man have to shut the door?
Why did Old Man and Old Woman laugh?

THE TALKING CROW

At one time there was a talking crow.

His name was Sim-sal-a-dim.

Day in and day out he sat

in a big green tree.

Day in and day out he called

from the tree,

"Sim - sal - a - dim.

Sim - sal - a - dim."

One day the farmer looked up in the tree.

"That crow talks all day long," he said.
"And all he can say is his name.
He just calls,

    'Sim - sal - a - dim.
    Sim - sal - a - dim.' "

The farmer's wife looked out
of the door.

"I will tell Sim-sal-a-dim
what to say," she said.
"He can do some work for me.
He can shoo the hens away
from my door."

The farmer's wife went to tell the crow
what to say.

She called to him,

"Shoo, shoo.
Go away.
Shoo, shoo."

Sim-sal-a-dim
looked down at her.
He called out,

"Shoo, shoo.
Go away.
Shoo, shoo."

"That is what I want you to say,"
said the farmer's wife.

Then she went back to work.

67

Shoo, Shoo

The next day some friends came
to see the farmer's wife.
She was not at home.

Sim-sal-a-dim called out,

"Shoo, shoo.
Go away.
Shoo, shoo."

He was in the big green tree,
but the friends did not see him.
They did not know who was calling.

Sim-sal-a-dim called again,

"Shoo, shoo.
Go away.
Shoo, shoo."

"Well!" said the friends.
"Someone is calling 'Shoo, shoo.'
So let's go."

At last the farmer's wife
came home.
She said, "My friends
came to see me.
But they went away.
Why did they go?"

Then she guessed what Sim-sal-a-dim
had said to them.

The farmer's wife looked out
of the window.
There was the crow
in the big green tree.

"Well!" she called.
"Do you know what you did?
You said 'shoo' to my friends.
So they went away.
The next time my friends come,
don't say 'shoo' to them.
Say,

'Do come in.
Do come in.' "

Sim-sal-a-dim

One day a man came to the door.
He was looking for something to eat.

Sim-sal-a-dim called down from the tree,

"Do come in.
Do come in."

The man looked all around.
Then he looked in the window.
No one was there,
so he went in.

71

When the man saw the food,
he sat down.

"Someone was calling to me," he said.
"Someone was calling 'Do come in.'
I guess someone wants me to eat
this food."

So he sat down to eat.

When the farmer and his wife came home,
they said, "Someone was here!"

The farmer looked at his wife.
He said, "Sim-sal-a-dim talked
to someone.
I know he did.
He said, 'Do come in.'
And now we have no food to eat."

The farmer and his wife ran out
of the door.

They saw the crow in the big green tree.

"I will tell him what to say,"
said the farmer's wife.

She called to the crow,

"Sim - sal - a - dim.

Sim - sal - a - dim."

The crow looked down at the farmer
and his wife.

"Sim - sal - a - dim," he called.

"Sim - sal - a - dim."

To this day that is all he will say.

Just his name.

So the farmer and his wife are happy.

Why are the farmer and his wife happy?

What would you tell the crow to say?

The Horse
with the Blue Tail

One day Horse looked around
and saw his tail.
"Oh my," he said.
"Where did I get this blue tail?"

Horse was happy with his tail.

Then Cat came around.

"I see that your tail is blue," said Cat.

"I am happy that my tail is not blue."

"Why do you say that?" asked Horse.

"Cats don't have blue tails," said his friend.

"Take a look around you.

Do you see other horses with blue tails?"

Horse looked all around.
"I guess there is no other horse
with a blue tail," he said.

Then he asked his friend,
"What can I do?"

"Well, I don't know," said Cat.
"But we will have
to think of something.
And soon."

So Horse and Cat
sat down to think.

Soon Cow came around.

"Good day to you," she said.

"It is not too good a day for us,"
said Cat.

"Look at Horse's blue tail."

"Have you had it long?" asked Cow.

"Where do you think you got it?"

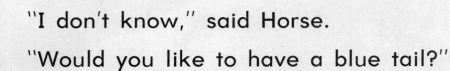

"I don't know," said Horse.

"Would you like to have a blue tail?"

"I would not," said Cow.

"A blue tail would not look too good
on me.

But I will sit down and help you
think of something."

So all three of them
sat down to think—
Horse,
Cat,
and Cow.

Think! Think!

The next one to come was Dog.

He was so happy that he was running and jumping all around.

"How are you?" he asked.

"Not too good," said Cow.

"Well, you three don't look happy," said Dog.

"Just look at my tail," said Horse.
"Can't you see that it is blue?"

"Yes, I see," said Dog.
"I like that blue tail.
How good it looks on you."

"The other horses don't have
blue tails," said Cat.
"What would you do
if your tail was blue?"

"I don't know what I would do,"
said Dog.

"Let me sit down with you.
I will see if I can help you
think of something."

So all four of them
sat down to think—
Horse,
Cat,
Cow,
and Dog.

Next, Bird came down from his tree.
He went up and down and all around.

"Stop, Bird! Stop!" said Cat.
"The four of us are thinking.
We can't think when you do that."

"Why do you have to think?" asked Bird.

"Just look at my tail," said Horse.
"There is no other horse with a blue tail."

"So what?" asked Bird.

"Well, how would you like to have a blue tail?" asked Cow.

"I wish I did have a blue tail," said Bird.

"Look at me.
I am all brown.
I like to see red birds,
and blue birds,
and yellow birds."

A Happy Horse

Horse did not want to be red.

He did not want to be blue.

He did not want to be yellow.

He wanted to be brown—all brown.

Horse was not happy.

Not happy at all.

Bird said, "Will your blue tail
stop you from eating?
Will it stop you from playing?"

"I guess not," said Horse.

"OK, Horse," said Bird.
"Now I will tell you something.
You can be happy if your tail is blue.
You can be happy if it is not blue."

"Well, I guess I can," said Horse.

"Then be happy!" said Bird.

Now Horse was happy.

He was so happy that he was running and jumping all around.

On all four of his feet.

Soon the farmer came.

He saw the blue tail on Horse.

Then he looked at the gate.

"That horse!" he said.

"What will he get into next?"

Why did the farmer look at the gate?

Will Horse's tail get to be brown again?

Why?

On Four Feet

Ping was a very big cat
and a very old cat.
He liked to sleep,
and sleep,
and sleep.

90

One day Ping was doing
what he liked to do—sleep.
Something hit him
on the head.
Something very big.

"Ouch!" said Ping.
"What hit me?"

There was Ling
on Ping's head.

Ling was a cat, too.

Ling had jumped out of a window
to get away from Stevie.

And now Ling
was on Ping's head.

"Ouch!" said Ping again.

"Go away!

I don't like to get hit
on the head."

Ling began to laugh.

He laughed
and he laughed.

"That was not funny!" said Ping.

"It was not funny to jump

out of the window.

And on my head.

So why are you laughing?"

"I will tell you," said Ling.

And he began to laugh again.

"OK," said Ping.

"Tell me what is so funny.

If you can stop laughing."

Ling

"Well," said Ling.
"I will tell you why I am laughing.
Stevie was at home with the sitter.
His mother was at work."

Ling began to laugh again.

"I don't see what is so funny,"
said Ping.
"Go on.
Tell me."

So Ling went on . . .

"Mark came to see Stevie.

He and Stevie played around.

Then they ran after me.

All around the room.

So I jumped up on a  .

Bang!

Down it went."

"I don't think that was funny,"
said Ping.

"No," said Ling.
"That was not very funny.
But let me tell you something
that was funny."

Then he said, "After that
the sitter came into the room.
She made Stevie stop
running around.
She let him pop some corn."

"Popcorn is good," said Ping.

"I had some," said Ling.
"Stevie and Mark thought I was funny.
All because I liked popcorn."

"Eating popcorn is funny

for a cat," said Ping.

"But not that funny."

"I know," said Ling.

"Stevie and Mark laughed
when they saw me eat.
They laughed because they thought
I was funny."

Ling laughed again when he thought
about Stevie and Mark.

"Well go on," said Ping.
"You always stop and laugh.
Tell me what Stevie did next."

So Ling went on . . .

"Stevie and Mark began to talk about cats.

Mark said that cats always land on four feet.

Stevie said he wanted to see if I would.

Then he came after me.

And I ran."

The Get Away

"Cats do land on four feet,"
said Ping.

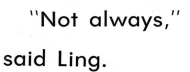

"Not always,"
said Ling.
"Some times I do.
Some times I don't.
This time I wanted
to get away.
So I ran fast.
Stevie came running after me,
and he hit something.
Down it went!"

Ping asked, "What went down?"

"The popcorn," said Ling.
"Stevie made the popcorn go down.
It went all over."

"I guess I know why you laughed,"
said Ping.

"No you don't!" said Ling.
"You just think you know."

Ling began to talk again.

He said, "I ran fast,
but Stevie got me.

He put me up
over his head.

Then he let go."

"What did you do?"
asked Ping.

"I came down,"
said Ling.

"On Stevie's head.

And I did land on my feet.

On all four feet.

Then Stevie had to go to his room."

"Why did Stevie have to go to his room?"
asked Ping.

"Because the sitter made him go,"
said Ling.
"I went to Stevie's room, too.
Then Stevie came after me.
But I jumped out of the window on you."

"That was not funny at all," said Ping.
"Not funny for me."

And he went
back to sleep.

Why did Ling laugh?
What would you do if a cat landed on you?

Do You Know?

1. What can go in a room with two legs and come out with six legs?

2. What do dogs have that cats do not have?

3. What can have a tail like a horse and not be a horse?

4. What dogs have no legs and no tails?

Popcorn

POP

POP   POP

Goes the popcorn.

HOP

HOP   HOP

Goes the popcorn.

TALK

TALK   TALK

Goes the popcorn.

All around
the pot.

Janet M. Perry
Age 8

How to Make Popcorn

This is what you do.

1. Put some cooking oil in a pan and heat the oil.

2. Put some popcorn in the pan and cover it.

3. Shake the pan and let the popcorn pop.

4. Put butter and salt on the popcorn.

Now you can eat the popcorn.

106

Tim Turtle

Rudy had a turtle that he got
from a pond.

He named him Tim Turtle.

Rudy liked to talk to Tim Turtle.

But every time Rudy talked,
Tim would pull his head in.

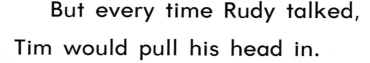

One day Rudy saw Tim Turtle
with his head out.

"Do you like this home, Tim Turtle?"
asked Rudy.

Tim Turtle did not talk.
He just pulled his head in.
That was his way of saying,
"No, I don't like this home.
I want to go back to my pond."

Rudy wanted Tim to eat something.
"Tim Turtle, eat this food," he said.
"It will be good for you."

Tim Turtle would not eat the food.
He just sat with his head pulled in.
That was his way of saying,
"I want to go back to my pond.
Take me home."

Rudy wanted Tim Turtle to be happy.

But all Tim would do was sit
with his head pulled in.

"Come on, Tim," said Rudy.

"Put your head out and swim."

But Tim Turtle did not want to swim.

He wanted to go back to his home
in the pond.

Rudy talked to Tim Turtle.

But talking did not make Tim happy.

He would not eat.

He would not swim.

All he would do was sit

with his head pulled in.

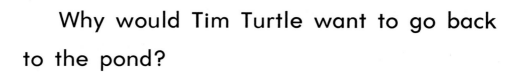

Tim Turtle wanted to go back

to his home in the pond.

Why would Tim Turtle want to go back
to the pond?

Help for Tim Turtle

Rudy could not think of a way
to make Tim Turtle happy.
So he went to see his mother.

"Tim Turtle is not happy," he said.
"I don't know what to do for him."

"I think Tim Turtle wants to go back
to the pond," said Mother.
"You could take him to the pond now.
See if he is happy there."

"I just wish Tim could be happy here," said Rudy.

"But I will take him to the pond."

Rudy put Tim Turtle into a box.

"Come on, Tim," he said.

"Do you want to go to the pond?"

Tim Turtle could not talk.

He just sat with his head pulled in.

Rudy took Tim Turtle to the pond.
When he got there,
he saw the trash.

"Oh, no!" he said.
"I don't want to put Tim
in that pond.
I will take him back home."

Mother saw Rudy when he came back from the pond.

He had Tim Turtle in the box.

Rudy did not look happy.

"I took Tim to the pond," he said.

"But I did not get near the water.

There is trash all around the pond.

I don't want to put Tim in the water because of all that trash!"

"No, that would never do," said Mother.

"What will we do about Tim?"
asked Rudy.

"He is not happy here.

He will not eat.

He will not swim.

He just sits with his head pulled in."

"Let's try to think of something,"
said Mother.

"I don't like trash near the pond.

And I don't like it in the water.

If we do something about the trash,
we will help Tim Turtle."

"Let's try to help him," said Rudy.

What do you think Rudy and his mother
could do?

At last Rudy thought he could put Tim in the water.

He wanted to see what Tim would do.

He wanted to see if he would be happy.

So Rudy got down near the pond and let Tim go.

Tim ran into the pond.

Well, he ran as fast as a turtle can run!

And this time his head was out.

How fast do you think a turtle can run?

Do you think Tim was happy to get back in the pond? Why?

TURTLES

Some turtles are very big.

They are so big that you could sit on them.

Some turtles never get very big.

They are so little that you could put them in your  .

Some turtles live in water.

Some turtles live on land.

Rudy's turtle lives in water.
It is called a red-eared turtle.
See if you can tell why.

A red-eared turtle will eat meat
when it is little.
It will eat plants when it gets big.

Some turtles eat meat
and plants.
Some turtles eat fish.
Some very big turtles
will eat birds.

Turtles can live for a long time
without food.

They do not come out to look for food
on cold days.

Why don't turtles come out
when it is cold?

What do you know about turtles now?

Do You Know?

1. What can you put up
   when the rain comes down?

2. What bird is always around
   when you eat?

3. What is black and white
   and red all over?

4. What do you have
   when you sit down
   but do not have
   when you walk?

Try, Try to Catch a Fly

"What is that?" asked Maria.

"A box," said her dad.

"I never saw a box like that," said Maria.

"What is it for?"

Dad laughed a little.

"I guess this box is funny looking," he said.

"But you can catch a fly in it."

"Catch a fly in a box?" asked Maria.
"That sure is a funny way
to catch a fly."

"I know it is," said her dad.
"But that is one way to do it.
Why don't you try to catch a fly
in this box?"

"I think I will," said Maria.

"Hey, Carlos," called Maria.

"Come over here and see this fly.

Just look at the way it walks.

It sure looks funny."

"What a way to walk!" said Carlos.

"On six legs.

Just think what you could do

if you had six legs."

"I could walk as fast as I can run now,"

said Maria.

"Take a look at the eyes," said Carlos.
"They sure are big."

"You know what?" asked Maria.
"A fly can see all around.
And up and down.
All at one time.
Dad said so."

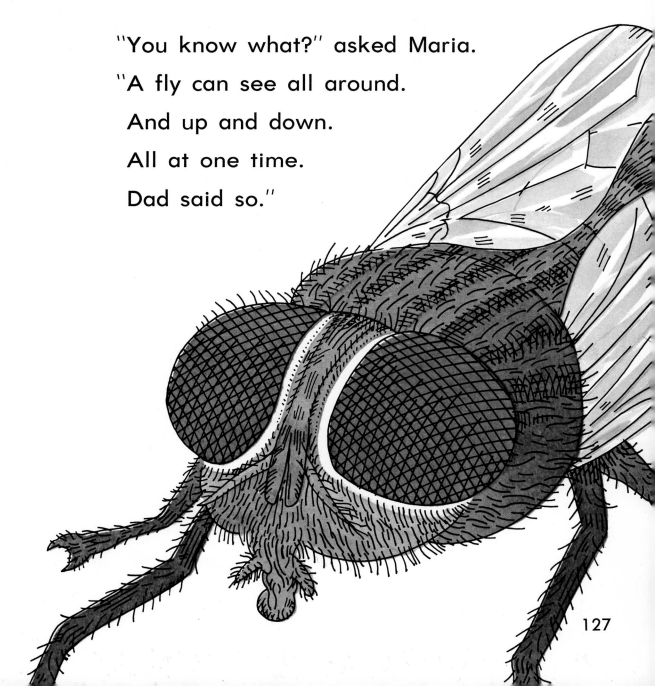

"It must be fun to have eyes
like a fly," said Carlos.

"You could see all around.
And up and down."

"Who wants eyes like a fly?"
asked Maria.

"Not me."

Do you think it would be fun
to have eyes like a fly? Why?

Other Ways to Catch a Fly

"Here comes a fly," said Carlos.

"Want to see me catch it?"

Maria said, "That was fun for you,
but it was not fun for the fly."

"Now we know two ways
to catch a fly," said Carlos.

"There must be other ways."

"Let's ask Dad," said Maria.

"He can tell us some other ways to do it."

Maria and Carlos ran to Dad.

"We know two ways to catch a fly," they said.

"Are there other ways to do it?"

"There sure are," said Dad.

"I can show you a plant that will catch a fly.

It will eat the fly, too."

"I never saw a plant that could eat a fly," said Maria.

"But I would like to see one that can."

"Me too," said Carlos.

Dad took Maria and Carlos
to see the plant.

Just before they went in,
Carlos saw something.

"Hey, come here," he called.

"I can show you a way to catch a fly."

"You are right," said Dad.

"A  can catch a fly."

Maria and Carlos and Dad began
to walk around.

They looked at all of the plants.

Before long Maria said, "Where is
the plant that can catch a fly?
That is what we came to see."

"It's right over there," said Dad.

Fly-Eating Plants

Dad took Maria and Carlos over to see the plant.

"How can that plant catch a fly?" asked Maria.

"I will try to show you," said Dad. "Let's take a look."

134

Maria and Carlos looked at the plant.

They wanted to see what it could do.

Dad said, "A fly will come to this plant
and land on it.

Then the plant will snap shut
and catch the fly."

"Can't the fly get out?" asked Carlos.

"No," said Dad.
"The plant will snap shut
before the fly can get away.
The plant snaps shut fast."

"Are there other plants
that catch flies?" asked Maria.

"There sure are," said Dad.
"Here are two of them."

"Now we know four ways to catch flies," said Carlos.

"I don't like flies around me," said Maria.
"Do you, Carlos?"

"No," said Carlos.

"Good!" said Maria.
"You say 'No.'
And so do I.
So let's try, try to catch a fly!"

What can you do to catch a fly?

Red Robin

Red Robin sat up in a tree.
He called,
  "Cheerily, cheer up,
  Cheerily, cheer up."
Again, and again, and again.

"Red Robin is asking for a wet head,"
said Sara's mother.

"That's why he sings."

"A wet head?" asked Sara.

"Why do you say that?

A robin can't ask for a wet head.

Red Robin can't talk!"

"No, Red Robin can't talk,"
said Sara's mother.
"But he can sing.
And now I think he is singing for rain."

"Why do you say that?" asked Sara.

"Well," her mother said,
"A robin that sings
Before going to bed
Will get up the next day
With a very wet head."

Red Robin called again,
  "Cheerily, cheer up,
  Cheerily, cheer up,
  Cheerily, cheerily."

"Stop that," said Sara.
"I don't want it to rain.
  Go to bed before you get
a very wet head."

"It's time that you were in bed, too,"
said her mother.
"You must go now."

The next day Sara looked for Red Robin.
He was not in the tree.

"Where can he be?" she asked.
She looked all around.
Then she saw him.

"You were right," she said.
"You were asking for a wet head."

Did Red Robin get a wet head?
How?

Why Robin Sings

Red Robin called from the tree,
"Cheerily, cheer up,
Cheerily, cheerily."

143

Sara said, "You were right, Red Robin.
It did rain.
And you did get a wet head."

"Do you always talk to birds?"
asked her father.

"Not always," said Sara.
"But sometimes it is fun to talk
to Red Robin.
He must know when it is going to rain.
That's when he sings."

"He sings at other times, too,"
said her father.

Then Red Robin began to sing,
  "Cheerily, cheer up,
  Cheerily, cheer up."

Sara's father looked up at Red Robin.
"Do you sing because you are happy?"
he asked.

Sara laughed.
"Look who is talking
to a bird now!" she said.

Red Robin called from the tree,

"Bup, bup.

Cuk, cuk.

Sssp, sssp.

Bup, bup."

Sara saw something run.

"My cat!" she said.

"Red Robin must see my cat."

"Bup, bup.

Cuk, cuk.

Sssp, sssp.

Bup, bup," called Red Robin.

"OK," said Sara.

"I will take my cat away."

Soon Red Robin called again,

"Bup, bup.

Cuk, cuk.

Sssp, sssp.

Bup, bup."

"Red Robin sees a bird,"
said Sara's father.
"I don't think he wants other birds
near his home."

"Why not?" asked Sara.

147

"Red Robin looks for food
near his home," said Sara's father.
"He wants all of the food.
For the little robins.
For Mother Robin.
And for Red Robin, too."

Why do robins call "Bup, bup"?
Why do robins sing "Cheerily, cheerily"?

Hop and Stop

Soon Red Robin came down
from the tree.
Sara looked at him.

First he would hop.
Then he would stop.
Then he put his head over
to one side.

"What now, Red Robin?" asked Sara.

"Red Robin is looking for food,"
said her father.
"That is why he hops and stops.
That is why he puts his head
over to one side."

Sara wanted to see
what Red Robin would do next.

First he would hop.
Then he would put his head over
to one side.
After that he put his head down
and began to pull at something.
It was a long brown 🪱.

"You were right," said Sara.

"That robin knows where the food is.

Mother Robin and the little robins

will be happy to see him."

How did Red Robin know
where the food was?

Why did he put his head over
to one side?

BIRDS

There are many, many birds.
Some birds get as big
as eight feet tall.

Some birds are so little
that you could put them in your  .

Some birds are called land birds.
They live in trees and on the land.

Some birds are called water birds.

Many of them live near the water.

Others live in the water.

Some water birds swim and fly.

But some water birds do not fly.

All they can do is swim and walk.

Some birds do not fly.
Some birds do not swim.

But all birds have two legs.
All birds have two  .
And all birds have feathers.

How many land birds can you name?

How many water birds can you name?

How many eyes do birds have?

What bird is eight feet tall?

A Robin

I wonder how
a robin hears?

I never yet
have seen his ears.

But I have seen him
cock his head,

And pull a worm
right out of bed.

Aileen Fisher

How to Make a Goofy Guitar

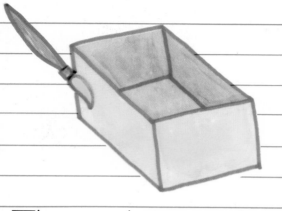

This is what you do.

1. Paint or color a shoe box.

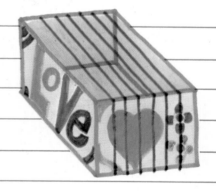

2. Make some pictures on the box.

3. Put six rubber bands around the box.

Now you can play your goofy guitar.

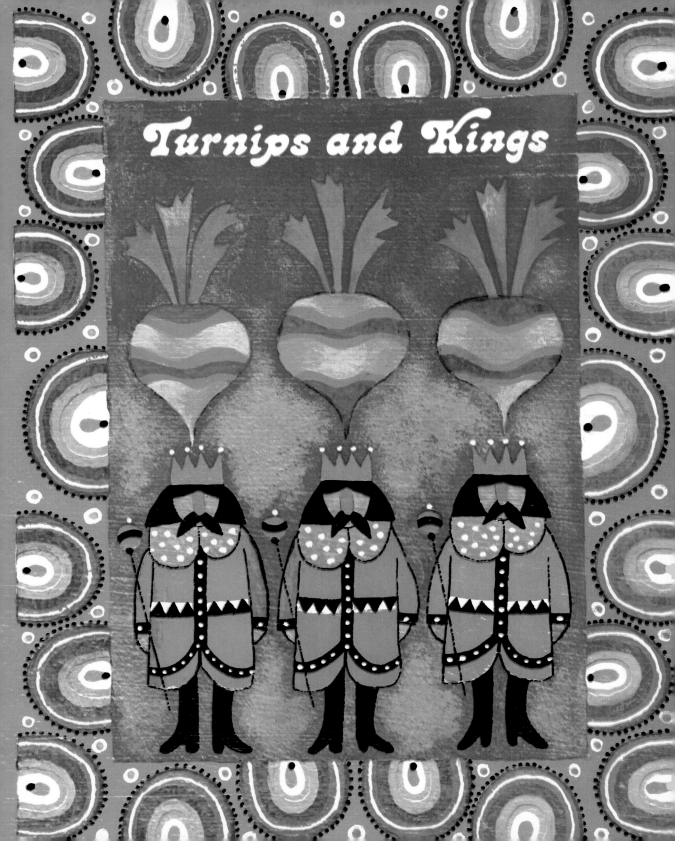

The Turnip

There once lived an old man
and an old woman.
They had a little white house
with tall trees all around it.

At one side of the little white house there was a garden.

Soon the days were not too cold. The old man and the old woman went out to their garden.

They thought they would plant a turnip in it.

They wanted the turnip to get big and tall.

So every day they wished for rain.

But the rain did not come.

159

"The garden must have rain,"
thought the old man.

"The turnip can't live without water,"
thought the old woman.

So every day they took water out
to their garden.

Every day they looked at their turnip.

All at once it began
to get big.

Before long, it was tall—
very tall.

The old woman said,
"Now I think it is just right.
Pull it out."

160

The old man gave the turnip a pull.

But the turnip would not come out.

He gave it a very big pull.

But the turnip would not come out.

The old man called to the old woman.

"Come here and help me," he said.

"This turnip is going to be hard

to pull out."

The old woman came
to help.

The old man pulled
at the turnip.

And the old woman pulled
at the old man.

They gave their turnip a pull.

But it would not come out.

"This is hard work," said the old man.

"Let's try to pull again."

So the old man pulled at the turnip.

The old woman pulled at the old man.

But the turnip would not come out.

Then the old woman called to a little girl.

"Will you help us pull this turnip out?"
she asked.

So the old man pulled at the turnip.

And the old woman pulled at the old man.

The little girl pulled at the old woman.

All three of them pulled.

But the turnip would not
come out.

"This is hard work," said the little girl.

She called to a boy, "Will you help us pull this turnip out?

It is very big."

So the old man pulled at the turnip.

And the old woman pulled at the old man.

The little girl pulled at the old woman.

The boy pulled at the little girl.

All four of them pulled.

But the turnip would not come out.

"This is hard work," said the boy.

He called to a cat, "Will you help us pull this turnip out?"

So the old man pulled at the turnip.

And the old woman pulled at the old man.

The little girl pulled at the old woman.

The boy pulled at the little girl.

The cat pulled at the boy.

And they pulled and they pulled.

But the turnip would not come out.

165

Then the cat called to a mouse.

"Will you help us pull this turnip out?"
she asked.

"It is very hard work."

So the old man pulled at the turnip.

And the old woman pulled at the old man.

The little girl pulled at the old woman.

The boy pulled at the little girl.

The cat pulled at the boy.

The mouse pulled at the cat.

And they gave one big pull.

And out came the turnip!

What will the old man and old woman
do with their turnip?

What would you do with the turnip?

Teeny-Tiny

Once there was a teeny-tiny woman.

She lived in a teeny-tiny house

in a teeny-tiny town.

One day the teeny-tiny woman
wanted to go for a walk.

So she put on her hat and went out
of her teeny-tiny house.

She thought she would take a walk
to the other side of the town.

The teeny-tiny woman walked over
to the other side of town.

All at once she saw a teeny-tiny gate.

She pulled the teeny-tiny gate
and walked into a garden.

She looked all around.

Then she saw a teeny-tiny bone.

"I can make something good to eat
with this teeny-tiny bone," she said.

So the teeny-tiny woman
took the teeny-tiny bone.
She shut the gate and went out
of the garden.
She walked back to her teeny-tiny house
on the other side of the town.

When the teeny-tiny woman got home,
she wanted to sleep.

So she put the teeny-tiny bone away
and went up to her teeny-tiny bed.
Soon the teeny-tiny woman
went to sleep.

Before long, a teeny-tiny voice called,
"Give me my bone!"

The teeny-tiny woman did not know
what to do.

She gave her bedclothes a pull.

Then she put her teeny-tiny head
under them and went back to sleep.

In a teeny-tiny time, the voice
called out again,

"Give me my bone!"

This time the voice was not so tiny.

Once again the teeny-tiny woman
gave her bedclothes a pull.

This time she put her teeny-tiny head
way down under them.

Soon she went back to sleep.

In a teeny-tiny time, the voice
called out again,

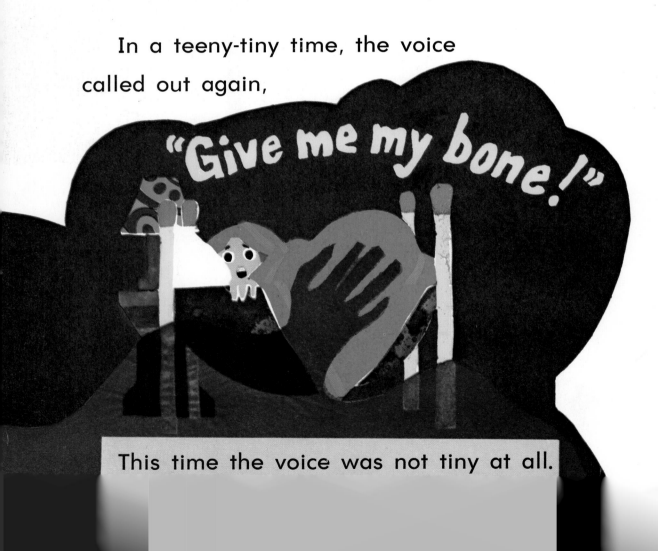

"Give me my bone!"

This time the voice was not tiny at all.

The teeny-tiny woman
could not sleep.

She pulled her head out
and looked under the bed.

Then she looked
all around the room.

She called back
in her very tiny voice,

"Take it!"

The teeny-tiny woman put her head
under the bedclothes again.

At last she could sleep.

There was no one to stop her.

Who called, "Give me my bone"?

Henny-Penny

One day Henny-Penny was in her garden
when something came down on her head.

"Oh, my!" she said.
"The sky is falling.
I must go and tell the king."

So she went along.

And she went along.

And she went along.

After a time she met Cocky-Locky.

"Where are you going?"
asked Cocky-Locky.

"Oh, I am going to town.
I am going to tell the king
that the sky is falling," said Henny-Penny.

"May I come with you?"
asked Cocky-Locky.

"Come along," said Henny-Penny.

So they went along.

And they went along.

And they went along.

And after a time they met Ducky-Lucky.

"Where are you going?"
asked Ducky-Lucky.

"Oh, we are going to tell the king
that the sky is falling," said Henny-Penny.

"May I come with you?"
asked Ducky-Lucky.

"Come along," said Henny-Penny
and Cocky-Locky.

So they went along.

And they went along.

And they went along.

And after a time they met Goosey-Loosey.

"Where are you going?"
asked Goosey-Loosey.

"Oh, we are going to tell the king
that the sky is falling," said Henny-Penny.

"May I come with you?"
asked Goosey-Loosey.

"Come along," said Henny-Penny,
Cocky-Locky, and Ducky-Lucky.

So they went along.

And they went along.

And they went along.

And after a time they met Turkey-Lurkey.

"Where are you going?"
asked Turkey-Lurkey.

"Oh, we are going to tell the king
that the sky is falling," said Henny-Penny.

"May I come with you?"
asked Turkey-Lurkey.

"Come along," said Henny-Penny,
Cocky-Locky, Ducky-Lucky,
and Goosey-Loosey.

So they went along.

And they went along.

And they went along.

And after a time they met Foxy-Loxy.

"Where are you going?"
asked Foxy-Loxy.

"We are going to tell the king
that the sky is falling," said Henny-Penny.

"But this is not the way to the king,"
said Foxy-Loxy.

"Do you want me to show you the way?"

"Oh, yes, we do!" said Henny-Penny.

"Come along then," said Foxy-Loxy.

So away they all went.

At last Foxy-Loxy said, "This is one way to get to the king.

I will go in first to show you the way.
You may come in after me."

So in he went.

But Henny-Penny said to her friends, "Don't go in.
Foxy-Loxy wants to eat us.
Run!"

They ran, and they ran, and they ran,
as fast as they could.
Back to the house
where Henny-Penny lived.

"Foxy-Loxy can't get us now,"
they said.

Whack!

Then
Something came down
near Henny-Penny's feet.
She looked at it,
and so did her friends.

"This is what hit me!" she said.
"It came down from that tree.
The sky is not falling at all!"

So they were all happy again—

Henny-Penny,

Cocky-Locky,

Ducky-Lucky,

Goosey-Loosey,

and Turkey-Lurkey.

And they did not have to tell the king that the sky was falling.

Do you think Foxy-Loxy was happy? Why?

Read All About It!

Big Turnip Comes Out

Woman Gives Up Bone

Henny-
Penny
Gets
Hit

Friends Help
Henny-Penny

Little Mouse Helps
in a Big Way

The Fox

In among the rocks
I found a little box.
And in the little box
There was a little fox.
He made a little sigh
And it almost made me cry.
He said although I'm sly
I wouldn't hurt a fly.

Margaret Hannon
Age 9

How to Make a Puppet

This is what you do.

1. Think about the puppet
   you want to make.

2. Lay the pattern on paper.
   Draw around the pattern.

3. Draw the puppet
   you want to make.

4. Cut out the puppet.

Now you can play
with your puppet.